The Heyday of the

BRITISH RAIL DIESELS

Paul Leavens & SVMRC

Once again we dedicate this album to those photographers of the railway scene of any era – thanks gentlemen!

ISBN 978-1-913049-01-0

Printed and bound by The Amadeus Press, Cleckheaton,West Yorkshire

Published by Book Law Publications, 382 Carlton Hill, Nottingham, NG4 1JA

Introduction

The so-called 'First Generation Diesels' basically started life in the 1955 British Railways Modernisation Plan. Looked at in depth – and hindsight – the plan was a massive gamble by a desperate punter! In parts the plan worked, in others it failed but overall it did what it was supposed to do and kicked started the modernisation of British Railways especially its huge, varied and ancient motive power fleet.

The purpose of this album therefore is to illustrate and comment on various aspects of the motive power in a critical but at the same time light-hearted way so as to inject some humour into a subject which over the last sixty-odd years has had some serious essays written about a period in BR history which was, frankly, not its finest hour.

There are no chapters as such but we have managed to group the images into a semblance which can hopefully be accepted by the reader. Regional groups are represented by the four found in England and Wales; Scotland has been left out of this one for reasons which will become apparent at a later date (no we are not waiting for Independence in order to create export figures from what is left of the United Kingdom).

Although the cover illustrations are in colour, black & white is the order of the day within the album. The mixture of images is exactly that and which will hopefully be to your liking. No matter where your allegiances lie, the presence of so many varied diesel images will please the eye.

We have drawn on two major collections to create this album and at the same time have been given help by a few other contributors on the way and for this we thank Roger Dring, and David Dunn.

David Allen, Newstead Abbey, Nottinghamshire, 2019.

(*Front cover*) 'Warship' D800 SIR BRIAN ROBERTSON glides beneath Mitre bridge near Old Oak Common in May 1960 with a Plymouth-Paddington express. *PL/BLP.*

(*Rear cover top*) BR Sulzer Type 2 D5103 departs from York with an Up express in September 1960. *PL/BLP.*

(*Rear cover bottom*) See page 92.

PLYMOUTH & ASPECTS OF THE WEST COUNTRY

(*above*) B-B 'Warship' D860 VICTORIOUS was delivered from North British in January 1962 and came complete with the four-aspect route indicator box at each end. This summer 1964 view at Plymouth's North Road station shows the diesel in harness with an unidentified sister. BLP. (*below*) Making its way to Laira depot after completion of duties, 'Western' D1051 WESTERN AMBASSADOR departs from North Road station on a damp April day in 1964. Passing the erstwhile North Road East signal box – given over to other purposes after the 1960 re-signalling – D1051 was by now a resident of Laira. However, the C-C started its career at Cardiff Canton in late January 1963, moving on to Old Oak Common on 29th September that year before transferring to 84A on 27th January 1964. *SVMRC.*

(*above*) One of Laira's B-B NBL Type 2s – D6303 – waits for a signal at Newton Abbot in May 1964. This locomotive was a member of a class which didn't really stand a chance in the scheme of things according to BR. For a start she was a diesel-hydraulic then she was one of those built in Glasgow by North British! Like the five NBL-built A1A-A1A 'Warships' the wheels of this class were for some reason spoked rather than solid disc wheels like the rest of the diesel fleet. It was as though NBL or the WR were trying to wrestle the last elements of steam locomotive design and include such with their diesel designs. (*below*) The retro-fitted route indicator boxes did little to enhance the ugly frontage of these 'Warships.' It might be considered that D602 BULLDOG has an appropriate name to go with the 'friendly' face! In case you didn't recognise the venue, it's Penzance and D602 is at the head of a Paddington working in 1966. *Both BLP*.

(*above*) Summer 1963 and 'Warship' B-B diesel hydraulics have started to take over the West of England-Waterloo expresses on account that the Western Region now stretches as far east as Salisbury along the former L&SW main line from Exeter. The Waterloo expresses are shared between SR Pacifics and WR diesels with the eventual dominance of the latter not too far away. This is 'Warship' D828 MAGNIFICENT – not really living up to its name – arriving at Exeter (Central) with the morning train from London. SVMRC (*below*) On the same day, sister D829 MAGPIE departs from Exeter (Central) for Waterloo with an all-Southern green rake of passenger vehicles to accompany its own green livery. The train originated in Exeter (St Davids) station and was brought up to its starting point by this Warship with the aid of a banker. *Both SVMRC*.

Look, no banker required! 'Hymek' D7085 ascends the incline from St Davids with a short train for Central in August 1964. Neither origin nor destination of this formation is known to this compiler. Suffice to say the Cardiff Canton B-B was looking rather grotty but a year in service on the Western without a wash was bound to show eventually. Cardiff 'Hymeks' were not too common a sight at Exeter and even more so at the top of the 1 in 37 incline. They were regular motive power on the Cardiff-Portsmouth trains which crossed the South Western main-line at Salisbury eighty-odd miles to the east! *SVMRC.*

D602's nameplate in 1966! H.M.S. BULLDOG was a wartime 'B' class destroyer – H91 – launched at Wallsend in December 1930. Before WW2 she was involved in the Arms Blockade imposed by Britain and France during the Spanish Civil War. She saw service evacuating British Army personnel – mainly 51st Highland Division – from Dunkirk, as an escort on the Atlantic convoys and then the Arctic convoys too. Bulldog was involved in what was to become one of the most secret operations of WW2 when escorting convoy OB318 she along with other escorts attacked and then captured U-boat U-110 a German type 1XB submarine in May 1941. From U-110 the boarding party from H.M.S. Bulldog retrieved an Enigma machine and code books, a secret maintained throughout WW2. Hollywood made a film of the action in 2000 but using American characters rather than British seamen whilst the submarine was designated U-571. The real U-110 sank whilst under tow back to Scapa Flow – the sub was allowed to sink in order to help preserve the secret – but the valuable code machine was soon to be safe at Bletchley Park. H.M.S. Bulldog was sold to be broken up for scrap on 15th January 1946. *BLP.*

DONCASTER & THEN DOWN THE ECML TO LONDON

(*above*) Having arrived at Doncaster new from Brush at Loughborough during late afternoon of Thursday 30th June 1960 Type 2s D5628 and D5629 joined the hundred-odd members of their class already earning a living on BR. It is now the following Monday – 4th July which for some reason is a big day in the United States of America – and the pair have just been out for a run to York and back and are seen to advantage from the footbridge spanning the lines from the station to the Plant works. (*below*) D5629 and D5628 making their way back into works to be stabled in the Paint shop yard where all new diesel locomotives were congregated every night during their acceptance trials. When they had completed those trials, the pair went their separate ways, D5628 to Ipswich and D5629 to March. *Both SVMRC.*

(*above*) Late August 1960, and EE Type 4 D286 thunders through Doncaster on the Down main with a northbound express; over near the works another newer but unidentified EE Type 4 is awaiting the acceptance trials team. It is late morning and Doncaster has plenty taking place. (*below*) BR Sulzer Type 4 D146 waiting for work at the north end of Doncaster station in April 1962. This Derby built main-line diesel was one of those which would become Class 46 under the TOPS scheme but in this view the locomotive was barely six months old and was on loan to Gateshead depot. The photograph was recorded during the period when diesel locomotives were being loaned out to all sorts of depots to see what would be best suited where. Of those which became Class 46 – D138 to D193 – many were sent out new for trial periods, of weeks or months, to Bristol Bath Road, Corkerhill, Darnall, Finsbury Park, Haymarket, Neville Hill, Newton Heath, St Rollox, Upperby. They didn't all get permanent allocations but many depots would be regularly receiving the type for servicing. The big winner was really Gateshead which between May 1962 and January 1963 received new examples D166 to D193 direct from Derby works. *Both SVMRC.*

(*above*) A busy time during the late morning! Passing Doncaster Carr with a Down express, Brush Type 4 D1527 overtakes Thompson B1 No.61196 on an empty mineral train whilst a BR Standard 9F awaits the signal. (*below*) 'Deltic' D9011 departs from Doncaster's platform 8 and runs onto the Down slow with an express for Newcastle in June 1962. The lines of vehicles outside the carriage works is a sight to behold with a variety never again to be gathered in one place. *Both SVMRC*·

(*above*) Following its younger and more powerful stablemate, EE Type 4 D245 hauls a Down express away from platform 8 at Doncaster in June 1962. The washing machine at Gateshead depot is certainly proving its worth! (*below*) Finsbury Park Brush 4 D1529 leaves Doncaster Carr locomotive shed behind as it hurries north with a fitted van train on a summer evening in 1963. *Both SVMRC.*

(*above*) York depot, it appears, did not have a washing machine for their diesel locomotives. D349 approaches Doncaster in 1963 with a northbound express. (*below*) This is one of the major morning expresses plying between Leeds (Central) and London (King's Cross). The date is sometime during summer 1965 and the motive power is Holbeck based Brush Type 4 D1570 which by any standards is atrocious. I can't remember if industrial unrest was a factor at the time. Or was the washer out of action? Indeed did 55A have a washing machine? Who was in charge? Who allowed this filthy machine to be coupled onto a prestigious express train from one of the UK's major cities and send it off to the capital? *Both SVMRC.*

(*above*) Garden sidings in summer 1964 with Finsbury Park 'Deltic' D9003 MELD heading a Down express. (*below*) Shortly afterwards another non-stop Down express with Gateshead charge D9005 THE PRINCE OF WALES'S OWN REGIMENT OF YORKSHIRE approaches St James's Bridge. The external appearance of the two 'Deltic's' is quite noticeable with the 52A locomotive showing the filthy livery for which Gateshead became infamous during BR days with its steam locomotive fleet; a sort of deja vu situation arose with the diesels too. Now Finsbury Park carried on with the same standards set at King's Cross Top Shed in the latter years of steam. *Both SVMRC*.

(*above*) The EE Type 3 was to become one of the most successful diesel locomotives to run on BR. Apart from its reliability it was extremely capable, and versatile. Here in June 1964 D6736 from Dairycoates heads an inter-regional fish train from Hull through a damp Doncaster. The main-line pilot is nowhere to be seen perhaps it had been called away? However, whatever problem was affecting Gateshead's cleaning routine was also spreading to Hull it seems! (*below*) Versatile: D6813 with a morning semi-fast on the Down main in 1963. *Both SVMRC.*

(*above*) EE Type 4 D207 has charge of a Down morning express at Doncaster in late August 1958 as steam still rules most of the BR network. The Type 4 was new from Vulcan Foundry the previous month and was the second of the batch allocated to Hornsey depot (D206 to D209) for exclusive use on the ECML – Stratford already had D200-D205 for GE Lines use – competing with the Pacifics. Initially the four worked between London and Edinburgh for just over a year before reinforcements arrived in the shape of sister D237 quickly followed by dozens of her ilk allocated to Gateshead, York and Haymarket. From D209's arrival in traffic during September 1958, BR did not purchase any more of the class until D210 was allocated to the LM Region in May 1959. This view of the main line south of St James's Bridge reveals Garden carriage sidings with a K3 and B1 in residence, and the Up goods yard with a diesel shunter in there somewhere! (*below*) Another aspect of D207 a few weeks later at the same place and again working a northbound express but this time on the Down slow. The top of the Up yard diesel shunter is discernible, just! *Both SVMRC.*

(*above*) Gateshead EE Type 4 D249 roars through Doncaster on the Up fast in May 1960 with an express for King's Cross shortly after midday. Note the main line pilot is a Peppercorn A1; that duty was going to remain steam hauled for many more years to follow. (*below*) Returning home! D249 waits at the signal near St James Bridge whilst working a Down express in 1960. Gateshead depot has attached a 52A shed plate to the cab side below the number at the No.1 end. Other depots located their shed plates in various places depending on the class of locomotive involved. In the previous image the shed plate was located beneath the number also at the No.1 end. *Both SVMRC.*

(*above*) D253 brings an express away from platform No.1 onto the Up main whilst steam locomotives hog the other trains in view. Note the deteriorating cleanliness of the York based Type 4 in this late September 1960 view. D253 went new to York on 8th January 1960 but a week later it went on loan to Leith Central which at that time was doubling up as Edinburgh's diesel depot. It returned to 50A on 19th March and had not been cleaned since it appears. (*below*) On Friday 26th May 1961 new production 'Deltic' D9003 heads a northbound express past Gardens carriage sidings where Gresley A3 No.60098 SPION KOP is readied for a run after completing a General overhaul at the nearby works. D9003 had been on BR metals since 27th March last and after its acceptance trials it was allocated to Finsbury Park from where it would operate for most of its life. In the July following this event being recorded, D9003 would be named MELD keeping alive a tradition that ECML express locomotives – like the A3 behind – were named after racehorses. *Both SVMRC.*

(*above*) It was 4A northbound (full) and A4 southbound (empties)! The daily Cliffe-Uddington bulk cement train and return empties brought a Southern Region BRC&W Type 3 onto the ECML as far as York where an EE Type 4 would usually take over. At York the Hither Green diesel would wait for the empties to arrive from Scotland and then return them to Kent; it was a slick operation which in the early days usually brought one of the Type 3s but after a series of failures en route, the train was given insurance in the shape of two SR Type 3s. This image from the summer of 1962 shows D6522 with the Down train passing Garden sidings; not only has the train got its usual complement of bulk tankers but this working has two suitably liveried vans containing hundredweight bags (112 lb.) – remember them? – of cement. (*below*) One of the pioneers of the EE Type 4s, D208, thunders through Doncaster with a lightweight – just eight bogies – express in April 1960. On the Up slow platform line what appears to be the Hull portion of *THE YORKSHIRE PULLMAN* is being propelled towards the Leeds portion prior to departure for the Capital. *Both SVMRC.*

(*above*) March based Brush Type 2 D5800 approaches Doncaster with a Down express in June 1964. Note the articulated twins behind the locomotive; are they from one of the LNER pre-war streamlined expresses? (*below*) D5800 again with what appears to be the Newcastle-Colchester passenger working in June 1964. Approaching St James Bridge this locomotive seems to have a panache for hauling unusual passenger stock because the vehicle immediately behind D5800 looks a bit Great Central? The Doncaster main-line pilot is still a steam locomotive note. *Both SVMRC.*

(*above*) Brush D1568 is approaching St James Bridge in late June 1964 with a Down express for Cleethorpes. This Type 4 was allocated to Immingham at this time. Just three months old, D1568 went new to Darnall on 28th March 1964 then to Immingham three weeks later. The relationship with the seaside was not going to last because in on 4th July next D1568 would be transferred to Finsbury Park for the remainder of the year. Although steam is still making its presence known, the carriage siding at the so-called Garden sidings are bereft of hauled stock and only a 3-car DMU is stabled; it's time to head south! (*below*) Late morning during a summer Saturday in 1964! Passing Babworth signal box near Retford, the Down working of *THE ANGLO-SCOTTISH CAR CARRIER* powers north behind a disappointingly filthy Brush Type 4 D1532 – at least the crew are wearing collars and ties. Whilst a steam-hauled freight waits in the Down loop, the crew of the yard shunter appear to have finished their shift and await the passage of the express so that they can book-off at the signal box. *Both SVMRC.*

(*above*) Babworth again but looking north now just a few minutes later when the Up working of *THE TEES-TYNE PULLMAN* was approaching the A620 road bridge. Hauled by Gateshead EE Type 4 D250 this train departed Newcastle at 0920, Darlington at 1006, and was due King's Cross at 1400. Note that D250 was wearing 52A's not quite unique livery of filth; even the locomotive's number is difficult to discern! Shunting a van train in the Up loop was a Brush type 4; now where was a shunter when you wanted one? (*below*) With hardly any clientele aboard, the late morning Down working of *THE MASTER CUTLER* negotiates the newly rationalised curve at Retford circa 1968 behind Tinsley Brush Type 4 D1510. Transferred from Finsbury Park to 41A in November 1967 along with a couple of dozen class mates, the Co-Co is wearing a 41A sticker on its cab side sheet just below its fleet number. The Pullman train was soon to switch to Sheffield's Midland station and then later use the Midland main-line to St Pancras; its short sojourn on the ECML was nearly over. *Both SVMRC*.

(*above*) Travelling another sixty-one miles south, we go back in time slightly to the late summer of 1958 to show Hornsey based EE Type 4 D208 running past New England yards with an Up express. (*below*) Traversing the girders of the Nene bridge just south of Peterborough with a scratch train of assorted but ancient rolling stock, EE Type 4 D207 heads south on a crew training trip to Hornsey in August 1958; this was probably one of the crew training specials from Sheffield which not only gave the footplate men an insight to the workings of the Type 4 diesel, but also the route along the ECML to KX which was new to them. Just weeks old, the big diesel was the second of her kind allocated to the ECML and being temporarily based at 34B. *Both SVMRC.*

(*above*) Wearing its 31B shed plate on its connecting door BR Sulzer Type 2 D5054 takes the route up to Crescent junction where it will join the ECML during summer 1960. One of sixty-one of her kind allocated new to March depot from new, D5054 arrived at 31B on 3rd December 1959. On 20th January 1961 the Bo-Bo transferred to Finsbury Park for a near six-year stint working the southern end of the ECML until called to Glasgow's Eastfield depot at the end of October 1966. Eighteen months in Scotland was enough for the Crewe-built diesel and in early April 1968 D5054 was sent to Manchester's Longsight depot to begin an eight-year long relationship with the LM Region. (*below*) With a service from Northampton to Cambridge, Stratford based Brush type 2 D5506 approaches Peterborough (East) in summer 1960 and is passing the former London & North Western Railway's long closed Peterborough Water End engine shed – the immaculate western light roof (a northlight but facing wet by necessity) still complete with smoke vents is nice to see after such a long absence of steam locomotives; the shed closed 8th February 1932 shortly after it was reroofed! The double track coming in from the right is the line from Crescent junction and the ECML. The Nene Valley Railway now occupies the track bed on which the Type 2 and its train was traversing. *Both SVMRC.*

(*above*) *THE MASTER CUTLER* again! D208 is doing the honours on the 1520 departure from Sheffield (Victoria) which is negotiating platform 2 at Peterborough (North) in 1960. (*below*) A near fifty-mile dash to the south brings us to Hatfield. After its station stop, this afternoon Down train to Hitchin powers away from Hatfield during the summer of 1959 with 'Baby Deltic' D5901 in charge. These Bo-Bos offered so much to the Eastern Region authorities; disappointment was however not on the list but that's what they got! *Both SVMRC*.

(*above*) An Up afternoon Cambridge express speeds through Hatfield in June 1959 with BRC&W Type 2 D5309 in charge. (*below*) A Down Cambridge express approaches Hatfield in June 1959 with Type 2 D5905 in charge. *Both SVMRC.*

(*above*) Finsbury Park's first 'Deltic' D9001 heads north through Potters bar in June 1961 with a Down express. The naming of this locomotive, which had been working since February last, was only weeks away. The chosen moniker was ST PADDY. It was the second of the class to be cut up, a deed carried out at Doncaster in February 1980; D9020 had been scrapped the previous month at 'The Plant' aged just short of eighteen! (*below*) Coming to a branch line near you! But only if you lived in Hertfordshire! This is BR Sulzer Type 2 D5069 on a summer morning in 1961 working one of the rubbish trains generated in London for land fill in Hertfordshire. The smell of this train on some days was quite potent according to those who experienced its passing. *Both SVMRC.*

(*above*) Heading into town in late 1961, during the morning rush! Brush Type 2 D5639 with a train which consisted a pair of Quad-Arts amongst its stock. (*below*) June 1961 and it's still going; a respectable looking EE Type 2 D5901 heads north with a morning local working through Potters Bar. *Both SVMRC.*

(*above*) One of the Cambridge expresses passing through Potters Bar in June 1961 with Brush type 2 D5602 in charge. (*below*) Having just traversed the longest tunnel on the ECML – Potters Bar 1214 yards – Gateshead EE Type 4 D248 makes light work out of this nine-car Down express on the climb to Potters Bar station on a glorious morning in June 1961. *SVMRC*.

(*above*) More Quad-Arts with Brush D5607 running on the Down slow through Potters Bar whilst heading for Hatfield. (*below*) Another rubbish train! An empty train of bogie mineral wagons is hauled south through Potters Bar in June 1961 by BR Sulzer Type 2 D5057. The Type 2 was new to March depot on 22nd December 1959 but transferred to Finsbury Park on 20th January 1961; their all-round versatility made locomotives in this class useful for most jobs such as this, suburban passenger trains, parcels trains, working engineers trains, and fitted freight trains. D5057 transferred on 13th August 1966 to the London Midland Western Lines at Willesden. *Both SVMRC*.

(*above*) It was a seemingly endless chain of King's Cross bound Quad-Arts during the morning rush. Finsbury Park's D5607 heads back into London through Potters Bar with its commuter train in June 1961. (*below*) An Up Cambridge at Potters Bar in June 1961 with D5602 in charge. *Both SVMRC.*

(*above*) Comparison time! A nice broadside of BRC&W Type 2 D5313 accelerating away after a stop at Potters Bar with a King's Cross bound local service on a summer evening in July 1959. This Bo-Bo was delivered new to Hornsey on 23rd January last although acceptance trials at Doncaster saw these delivery dates extended by a week or so. When the new depot at Finsbury Park became operational from 24th April 1960 all the main-line diesel locomotives residing at Hornsey shed were transferred en masse to 34G. However, this particular Type 2 and her sisters – D5302-D5317 – were transferred to the Scottish Region at Haymarket on 18th and 19th June 1960. D5300 and D5301 had gone north in March as the advance party whilst D5318 and D5319 joined the rest at 64B on 9th October 1960, bringing up the rear-party so to speak! The Eastern Region had lost some superb reliable locomotives but part of the deal must had included the North British Locomotive Co. built Type 2s D6100 to D6137 also being accepted by ScR because between 16th April and 11th September 1960 those locomotives were transferred north from the following depots: Hornsey and Finsbury Park D6100-D6109; Stratford D6110-D6119; Ipswich D6120-D6129 and D6131-D6137 (D6130 had moved to Eastfield 14th November 1959). As we can recall, the Scottish Region got the worst of the deal with the NBL Type 2s being amongst the worse locomotives ordered under the 1955 Modernisation Plan. (*below*) With bits of newness still apparent, D5904 runs through Potters Bar in July 1959. *Both SVMRC.*

(*above*) Working a commuters train to Hatfield BRC&W Type 2 D5317 heads north through Potters Bar in July 1959! (*below*) Another evening northbound local works through Potters Bar in July 1959 with 'Baby Deltic' D5901 in charge. This Bo-Bo was new to Hornsey on 22nd May last. *Both SVMRC*.

(*top*) 'Peak' D168 joins the Down main at Wood Green with a fitted freight on 16th March 1963. New to Gateshead less than ten months previously, the big diesel has taken on the 52A persona. *PL/BLP*. (*centre*) Type 2 D5639 waits to join the main line at Wood Green for the trip down to King's Cross with a train of Quad-Arts on Saturday 7th October 1961. *PL/BLP*. (*above*) Early start; King's Cross with D5645 and D5612 on an unknown date in 1961. *SVMRC*.

(*above*) New on the property! Brush Type 2 D5643 stands at the head of suburban stock in platform 12 at King's Cross in September 1960. *SVMRC*. (*below*) Doyen of the BRC&W Type 2s D5300 heads an evening Cambridge service at King's Cross in October 1958. Allocated to Hornsey when new on 30th July 1958, this member of the ER fleet never did get to use the facilities at Finsbury Park as in company with sister D5301, they formed the advance party of the mass transfer to Scotland and by the end of March 1960 were resident at Haymarket depot. *PL/BLP*.

(*above*) D207 at King's Cross 1959. (*below*) Gateshead 'Deltic' D9005 THE PRINCE OF WALES'S OWN REGIMENT OF YORKSHIRE departs from King's Cross with a Down express in 1966. *Both PL/BLP*.

ON SHED - A REAL MIXED BAG!

(*above*) A quiet Sunday at Lincoln circa 1965 with one of Tinsley's vast fleet of Brush Type 4's stabled for the weekend along with two other 41A charges, Brush Type 2s D5831 and D5824. *BLP*. (*below*) Sharing the premises at King's Cross 'Top shed' October 1961. Even though Finsbury Park was operational having diesels in town was obviously desirable. The great curving site occupied by King's Cross engine shed put this row of buildings on the north side of the shed block. The two right-hand roads constituted the first rudimentary diesel shed at 34A. *PL/BLP*.

D220
865

(*opposite*) EE Type 4 D220 was released new to BR from Vulcan Foundry on Friday 17th July 1959 and after a week or so running acceptance trials it was allocated to Crewe North. It was from 5A that the big diesel worked an express to London (Euston) from where it was sent to Camden 1B for servicing prior to returning home. In this view D220 has just come on shed and is about to reverse onto the stabling road on the left of the image. Steam locomotives had to negotiate the turntable, visit the coal and ash plants, and then fill up their tenders with water before returning to this location where they could then reverse onto a shed road; complicated? More like time consuming but the best that could be had from the shed layout. Back to our subject; D220 was named FRANCONIA on 16th February 1963 by which time that little ladder fitted to the front of the nose would have disappeared. (*above*) Camden shed when the diesels had become a little more established but steam still ruled. D228 was running onto a shed road after working light up Camden bank from the terminus. (*right*) 'Peak' D7 INGLEBOROUGH stabled at the top end of Camden's yard in July 1960 – note THE RED ROSE headboard plate on the buffer stop. Recorded as being allocated new to Camden on 28th November 1959, D7 was instead 'on loan' to Derby 17A shed for evaluation of the class in general. It eventually reached 1B on 23rd April 1960 and remained working the WCML rails for two years until it was transferred to Toton 18A and a lifetime of freight haulage. When she was discarded, she was the last of the original ten to be cut up, a deed which took place at Derby in November 1981 some twenty-two years to the day when she was originally allocated to 1B! *All SVMRC.*

(*above*) Hudswell Clarke 0-6-0 Diesel Mechanical D2518 inside a well-illuminated Willesden roundhouse on 24th March 1963. The little shunter was some eighteen months old by now, but was looking remarkably smart, so was probably one particular Drivers' regular engine. Initially allocated new to Watford 1C on 25th November 1961, it transferred to Willesden 1A on 5th January 1963. On Bonfire night 1966 it was transferred to Crewe from where it was withdrawn on 25th February 1967 as surplus. It was sold to the National Coal Board at Hatfield Main Colliery near Doncaster. Note the 1A shedplate on the door! For the modellers amongst you note also the heat reflective plate retro-fixed to the top of the engine cowling. PL/BLP. (*below*) Hunslet 0-6-0 DM twins D2593 and D2603 outside the repair shop and stores block at Ardsley shed on 6th September 1964. N.W.Skinner (*ARPT*).

Clean, dirty! (*above*) Ex-works BR Sulzer Type 2 D5178 at York depot on Wednesday 20th October 1965 in company with sister D5177. The pair had just been transferred from Gateshead 52A to York 50A the previous day, our subject here straight after a period in Darlington works receiving a major overhaul and repaint. (*below*) D5177 stands alongside a former steam locomotive tender converted into a water carrier for the Chief Civil Engineer West Riding District. Another former Midland Railway locomotive tender – still carrying the old BR emblem – is coupled. Note the buffers retro-fitted to the former working end of the tender. D5177 ex-52A what can we say? One out of two ain't bad! Both of the BR Sulzer Type 2s had followed each other around the NE Region to date. From new at Darlington in February 1963 they went to Holbeck but later transferred to Gateshead. From York they moved to Thornaby but that's another tale. *Both BLP.*

(*above*) When they were new! Well two months old. Crewe-built Brush D1100 stabled at York with older sister D1588 – Crewe May 1964 – in September 1966. (*below*) BR Sulzer Type 2 D5101 at York in 1966 with resident EE Type 4 D387. Although looking brand new, D5101 had in fact been built – Darlington 9th July 1960 – long before the Vulcan Foundry built Type 4 entered traffic – 11th April 1962 – so what we see here is one of those 'ex-works after a major overhaul images!' At the time the Type 2 was allocated to Gateshead and was on its way back home from the locomotive works at Derby. Both locomotives in this image would transfer not too long afterwards: D5101 to Holbeck on 7th October 1967 and D387 to Healey Mills in September 1966. When 52A handed over D5101 to 55A in 1967 it would look nothing like this having accumulated over a year of filth. *Both BLP*.

(*above*) Brush D1999 inside a dilapidated York engine shed in 1966. The final ten of the main number group were all allocated new to York from their maker at Crewe in 1966. To follow on, the final dozen – D1100 to D1111 – were also built at Crewe and supplied to 50A between July 1966 and February 1967 (see opposite). BLP. (*below*) EE Type 3 D6740 was new to Hull Dairycoates depot (50B) on 1st June 1962. This image dated 19th August 1962 shows the still clean diesel-electric stabled for the weekend at Normanton engine shed (55E) when steam still ruled around those parts! Dairycoates initially had a dozen of these Type 3s allocated – D6730 to D6741 – arriving new from Vulcan Foundry during the period 16th October 1961 to 7th June 1962. Another smaller batch – D6779 to D6783 – from the Robert Stephenson Hawthorn works at Darlington turned up later during November and December 1962. *C.J.B.Sanderson (ARPT)*.

Just when you thought it had gone all-diesel, the preserved steam gate-crashed an otherwise tranquil scene! This is Swindon running shed 82C on 29th day of May 1965 with two visiting steam locomotives on show. The boiler of 4472 FLYING SCOTSMAN is partly visible; the Pacific had arrived in Swindon that very day on a rail tour whereas No.4079 PENDENNIS CASTLE was apparently awaiting a call to perform such a duty. Of the diesels only the following are noted: D1811, D7012, D7041; the unidentified D95XX 0-6-0DH with yellow painted buffer beam was possibly a new example which was yet to be allocated. At this period in time Swindon still had to turn-out eleven more of the class to complete so this one could be D9544 allocated to Cardiff Canton and which would be withdrawn less than three years later from Hull Dairycoates its last BR shed where thirty-three of the original fifty-six ended up! D9544 was sold on to British Steel Corporation at Corby who managed to employ the locomotive for twelve years – so they got a bargain! *PL/BLP*.

(*above*) Two of the early Swindon-built B-B 'Warships' D807 CARADOC and D804 AVENGER alongside the fuelling racks at Old Oak Common depot circa October 1959. PL/BLP. (*below*) Laira depot circa May 1965 with two of their A1A-A1A 'Warships' – D600 ACTIVE and D602 BULLDOG – looking rather neglected. Quoting the WR Traction Controller, Paddington – also a long standing RCTS member – from the March 1968 issue of the Railway Observer talking about the five 'Warships' D600-D604 "These locomotives like most other diesel types (particularly hydraulics) gave a fair amount of trouble when new and for some time afterwards in this case. I agree that some in particular have spent longer spells than usual in Works. However those in service at Plymouth (generally four or five per day through most of last summer and autumn until the transfers too place [to Landore]), their performance was no worse and no better than other locomotives over the same route. They were allocated [work] with discretion when it came to the heavier trains but the Down 'Limited' was quite often entrusted to them. With regard to the withdrawal of these locomotives the fleet was being reduced and the elimination of a non-standard class with the associated savings in stores, etc., was considerable." So there you have it! Note the position of the 84A shed plate on the lower front fairing. *BLP*.

(*above*) A general view of the siding at Laira with the two larger 'Warships' stabled in May 1965 along with B-B D803 ALBION. Note that D600 has yet to receive those split box route indicators. The drive-through locomotive washing machine on the left of this image must have been broken as none of the locomotives in view have been driven through for some time. I forgot to mention that for the final two years of their lives, D600 to D604 were banned from working east of Plymouth because the Laira fitters were then able to repair them anywhere in Cornwall.
(*below*) BR Type 1 Class leader D9500 was allocated to Bath Road shed 82A at Bristol when new – 8th July 1964 – but on 20th May 1967 it transferred to Cardiff Canton 86A (on paper) prior to its redundancy and periods in store. On an unknown date in late 1964, the 0-6-0DH stands on shed with 'Warship' D841 ROEBUCK whilst displaying its Swindon Built 1964 plate above its A82 shed plate. The fleet number D9500 is not displayed in one of the accepted fonts of the period and once again spoked wheels are rampant! They liked to be different on the WR, buck trends, and ignore convention, not to mention the waste of money! It was reported that D9500 and D9531 were taken from Bristol to Shrub Hill goods shed in Worcester during December 1967 where they were sheeted over; D9500 never did get to Cardiff. *Both BLP*.

DELTIC PROTOTYPES 1 & 2:

(*top*) During the period in railway history when the Sheffield Pullman or to give it its official name *THE MASTER CUTLER* used to ply between Sheffield (Victoria) and London (King's Cross), it made the return journey some twice a day. The train had been relaunched in September 1958 with diesel haulage and somewhat faster timings to the Capital via the ECML rather than the original once daily journey over the former Great Central route to London (Marylebone). The original motive power comprised English Electric Type 4s but from about 1960 uprated Brush Type 2s – amongst others – took on the duties. However on this occasion, here at Woodhouse just after noon on a sunny day circa 1963, the Down morning service (1120 ex-King's Cross) was composed of seven Pullmans and a single Mk.1 full brake, being hauled by DP2. (*above*) DP2 returns to London with the afternoon (1520 ex-Victoria) Up working of *THE MASTER CUTLER*. The chances were that DP2 would not return to Sheffield with the Down (1920 ex-KX) working of this train which was then entrusted to another locomotive. DP2 was probably going to take part in a Diagram which would see it haul a service to Newcastle as the first part of what was quite an extensive diagram for the locomotive which would see a mileage exceeding 4,500 miles a week. Once again the photographer captures the train at Woodhouse but this time just west of the station at the very edge of the Manchester, Sheffield, Wath electrification territory. *Both SVMRC.*

According to the Locomotive Works clock the time was 1215 but alas we have no date for this image. However, summer 1960 might be a good guess; it is sunny, trees are in full bloom, and a new EE Type 4 fresh from Vulcan Foundry is having acceptance trials. 'Deltic' herself is stabled in bay platform 2 and is quietly attracting attention from the assembled railwaymen. Little did those footplatemen know at the time but before the full complement of EE Type 4s was delivered, the production batch of twenty-two 'Deltics' would start arriving at the place which would look after them for the next twenty-odd years. *SVMRC.*

(*above*) DP2 again but somewhat cleaner on 15th July 1963! This time the one-off was working an express from London (King's Cross) to Leeds (Central) and was just passing Copley Hill engine shed whilst crossing over the thoroughfare of the same name as it neared its destination. Approaching from the east was 'Britannia' Pacific No.70041 SIR JOHN MOORE with an Up express. *Malcolm Foreman*. (*below*) The 'Deltic' making its way out of King's Cross terminus on a sunny summer evening in 1959. Signalled for M2 – Main 2 – the big diesel was en route to Hornsey where it would refuel and spend the night before taking on another load of work the following day. The staff sat taking a break beneath the signal box steps haven't given the locomotive a second glance as they had seen it all before. *SVMRC*.

(*above*) She must have been quite an 'eye-opener' to everyone when released onto BR metals during the austere Fifties' when anything colourful attracted attention. From this aspect even those cheat lines with their pointed ends look just right, and as for those portholes in the doors! Here the lady is apparently at Retford on express duties. (*below*) Even 'Deltic' required water! At least for the train heating boiler and here at Doncaster during the summer of 1959 the Co-Co is drawn up alongside the water column located between the Up fast and the Up slow line serving platform 4. Note the 40-gallon oil drums on the platform and more of the same on page 46! *Both SVMRC*.

THE LMR & THE WCML

(*above*) Although this image is slightly damaged, it is included simply for its rarity value. It features the first 'Peak' D1 SCAFELL PIKE at the head of an Up express at Manchester (Central) in 1959. At the time the 'Peak' was still showing signs of newness from its April date into traffic but that wouldn't last much longer. Allocated to Derby for evaluation, D1 was, on paper, allocated to Camden for trials on the WCML as were its nine sisters but it was August 1959 before the big diesel transferred from the Midland Lines to Western Lines control. So, views such as this showing one of the ten working an express passenger train on the Midland Lines is quite rare because once their work on the WCML was done, they all moved to Toton from where the working of freight trains became their lot! (*below*) Wembley carriage sidings: no date for this image but both items of motive power were visitors to this location. The Brush Type 4, D1524, was one of the Finsbury Park fleet and wears the 34G shed plate on its front panel just below the route indicator; it appears D1524 has worked in on a special – 3X23. The Midland Pullman set has worked down from Manchester – which station? – as 1X70, another special working; its home depot Reddish have done an excellent job cleaning the bodywork; now what was the occasion; the date would clinch it surely! *Both PL/BLP.*

(*above*) Bulwell Common, Nottingham 12th August 1965 when coal was king and every other train around here it seemed was moving the stuff; the others were just empties returning to the pits for more coal! BR Sulzer Type 2 D5293 has charge of a southbound load whilst towards the station in the background a WD 2-8-0 is working onto the main line with another load of black diamonds. The sidings on the Down side contain empty mineral wagons en route to a nearby colliery. This is the former Great Central main line which – on the north side of the city – was duplicated twice by the Great Northern Railway and the Midland Railway routes which also served the local coal mines. The sandstone outcrops usually give a clue as to the riches which lie beneath your feet. *PL/BLP*. (*below*) Derby based 'Peak' D38 heads an inter-regional express through Burton-upon-Trent in June 1963. *SVMRC*.

(*above*) This page is not dedicated to the less than successful designs of BR diesels it just happened to fall that way! Metrovick Co-Bos D5700 and D5701 enter St Pancras on an unknown date but circa July 1959 with an express from the East Midlands. The class were no strangers in London but they didn't normally penetrate this far into the city usually being confined to Cricklewood for working the *CONDOR* overnight freight to Glasgow. (*below*) Caught on the Settle & Carlisle line near Ais Gill on 20th August 1963, new Clayton Type 1s D8540 – leading – and D8526 make their way towards Glasgow. They certainly look smart in their two-tone green livery (so that's where Swindon got the idea from!) but hindsight tells us that not all was how it appeared. *Both PL/BLP*.

(*above*) When the diesels arrived at Toton, many of their ilk were consigned to working the coal trains being supplied by the mines situated in Sherwood forest and which were sunk during the Grouping period when both the LMS and LNER were involved in shifting the coal produced. The collieries were very productive compared with those older pits in the surrounding coalfields. On 13th August 1965 Brush Type 4 D1823 was being piloted by Stanier 8F No.48643 through the maze of single lines running through the forest as here at Rufford Junction. Clipstone Colliery is just discernible in the centre background. (*below*) In today's parlance this would be treated as a 24/6 operation or to be more accurate 24/5.5 with the continuous movement of coal from the most productive collieries served providing almost two million tons each at the surface every year. This is Toton based D1618 being piloted by 8F No.48442 near Rufford on 12th August 1965. *Both PL/BLP*.

(*above*) Another steam/diesel combination, this time with D1836 piloted by 8F No.48334 exiting Kirkby tunnel on 14th May 1965. The steam locomotives were provided to give the diesels additional braking power throughout their journey from the mines but especially during the descent from Kirkby Summit junction to Pinxton. (*below*) A Clipstone-Kirkby train runs into the morning sun with 8F No.48364 piloting atrocious looking Brush D1617 with a heavy train on 14th May 1965. These forest railways served the pits at Bilsthorpe, Blidworth, Clipstone, and Rufford. *Both PL/BLP*.

(*above*) Starting to muscle in on the WCML express passenger work during the summer of 1959, the EE Type 4 fleet belonging to the LMR was growing weekly. This is D212 winding-up a late afternoon Down express after the toil of Camden bank. (*below*) With three 350 h.p. diesel-electric shunters working Camden goods yard and BR Sulzer Type 2s on empty stock duties from Euston – D5077 – you would think that diesel had taken over the operations at the south end of the WCML but that was a few years off yet. *Both SVMRC*.

(*above*) New EE Type 4 D218 runs into Camden from the north with an assortment of empty coaching stock forming a lightweight load for a training run in late July 1959. At that time D218 was allocated to Crewe North – new 11th July 1959 – but would move on to Edge Hill on 8th August before settling at Longsight on 10th September 1960 where it was named CARMANIA on 12th July 1961. (*below*) Another view of D218 at a later date but at virtually the same place and viewed from a different aspect. It is still the height of summer but the evening sun is casting longer shadows whereas the Type 4 is looking extremely grubby. A Watford line train is just emerging from the underpass beneath the main line. *Both SVMRC.*

Working the 1750 Down service of *THE MANCUNIAN*, Longsight's newly acquired EE Type 4 D225 is passing sister D220 and a few more of their kind resident on Camden shed in June 1960. The continuing procession of locomotives coming up from Euston for servicing is evident as another Type 4 runs past the shed in the wake of D220. The Class 5 on the turntable is proof of the steam presence here along with a couple of 'Royal Scots' already serviced and tucked-up on shed. D225 and her express were due into Manchester at 2140. *SVMRC*.

Just a little earlier than the Manchester express this local commuter working to Bletchley came up Camden bank and took the Down Watford electric line with former S.R. Type 4 design 10203 in charge. This locomotive and its twin sisters epitomised the 'box' description so beloved by all those steam enthusiasts who had little time for the BR diesel fleet. 10203 and her two similar but older sisters were transferred from the SR to the LMR in 1955 and settled down on main-line expresses out of Euston and in between took on work such as this. From 1962 onwards the trio began long periods in store as the EE Type 4 fleet took over much of the main-line work alongside the steam Pacifics. In 1968 all three were condemned and then sold off to a private scrapyard in Great Bridge. *SVMRC.*

(*above*) With the summer sun in setting mode, BR Sulzer Type 2 D5074 returns to Euston with a now fairly empty commuter train. Below it, a Watford line electric unit is doing the same thing. The type 2 started life at March depot in the Fens on 14th March 1960 but two weeks later it was transferred to the LMR and Willesden in particular along with dozens of its sisters which were cleared out of 31B. In this July 1960 image, D5074 was still a Willesden engine but during the coming November it transferred to Watford for a two month stint before returning to 1A. (*below*) Straight out of the Meccano factory at Binns Road, Liverpool! This is the Hornby-Dublo Type 1 as first produced in OO gauge. Considering it was so long ago, Meccano made a pretty good job of that model and of course they were brave enough to produce a diesel prototype at a time when many rail enthusiasts had layouts but were anti-diesel if you can believe such a thing! This is the real EE Type 1 1,000 h.p. diesel-electric D8044 on shunting duties at Camden goods yard in July 1960. Commuters on Primrose Hill station platforms must have been thinking "That's that Hornby diesel over there!" At the time D8044 was resident at Devon's Road, Bow after a period on loan from Norwich Thorpe where she went new on 24th November 1959. Willesden acquired the Bo-Bo on 21st April 1962. *Both SVMRC*.

(*above*) Our last look at Camden and we finish with this dramatic image of EE Type 4 D234 turning into the sun with a Down express in 1960 and viewed from the wall running along King Henry's Road, Primrose Hill. SVMRC. (*below*) Making our way north, we stop off at Bushey water troughs on 27th July 1963 with EE Type 4 D374 dipping it's train heating tank water scoop whilst working an afternoon express. Perhaps the dip was an exercise to keep the Fireman 'up-to-scratch' or perhaps the crew had been given word that the temperature was going to drop before the train reached its destination? Readers! The choice is yours! *PL/BLP*.

(*above*) It looks as though the Driver has got the Secondman sitting at the controls of EE Type 4 D337 hauling the eight-coach Down service of the *ROYAL SCOT* through Leyland in August 1961. Departed London (Euston) 0950, due Glasgow (Central) 1745. (*below*) Our old friend D227 again and this time working a Whitehaven-London express near Leyland in August 1960. The big diesel has yet to acquire the yellow painted warning panel on the front and those miniature ladders still adorn the nose! In the background Lostock Hall engine shed is busy as are the cotton mills surrounded by terraced housing. *Both SVMRC.*

(*above*) On an Up Anglo-Scottish express this time, yes its D227 again but in late summer 1959 when it was still fairly new; note the reflective surface of the bodyside. We are at Carnforth where steam is naturally ruling the roost. (*below*) In August 1960, one of the original 'Peaks' D7 INGLEBOROUGH accelerates away from Carnforth after taking over an empty stock working which had originated on the Cumbrian coast. At this time the big diesel was allocated to Camden shed and not even a year old, note how grubby D7 has become. The external condition of the trailing load also leaves a lot to be desired. *Both SVMRC.*

The classic view of Dent station with an unidentified 'Peak' passing on a damp Wednesday, 21st August 1963. *PL/BLP*.

(*above*) The Crewe works test train near Low Gill in May 1964 with nearly completed Brush D1597, still in primer, showing off with fifteen on! (*below*) A rather smart looking EE Type 4 – D308 – shuts off the power and begins the coast down to Tebay with an Up express during the evening of Wednesday 1st August 1963. *Both PL/BLP*.

IN & AROUND SHEFFIELD, ROTHERHAM & THEN SOUTH TO DERBY

(*above*) In the days when it was still running to King's Cross but not from Sheffield (Victoria), the morning service of *THE MASTER CUTLER* waits on platform 1 at Sheffield (Midland) behind Brush D1704. The north facing start would take the train to Nunnery curve where it would ascend the short incline up to the former GCR route where it would then resume its usual course via Retford and the ECML. (*below*) With some specialist wagons in tow, Darnall based Brush D5691 runs east through Woodhouse and leaves the electrified area of Sheffield behind in May 1962. *Both SVMRC.*

(*above*) During a lovely morning in September 1962, one of Darnall's numerous Brush Type 2s, D5847, rounds the curve at Masboro' Station South Junction with a northbound working. The train is coming off the former Sheffield & Rotherham Railway onto North Midland metals. (*below*) EE Type 1 D8096 shunting at Rotherham Masboro' Station South Jct. signal box in September 1962. Note those Hornby style ladders attached to the bodyside. In the right background a number of trains are awaiting paths with north and east bound freights in the goods yard. *Both SVMRC.*

It was a busy morning; in fact it was busy all the time here it seems. 'Peak' D129 and another northbound passenger working negotiates the Masboro Station South Junction in September 1962. In the background the steel mills of Rotherham form an unbroken line of industrial premises. Now, I wonder how many of the regulars' at The Red Bull were enthusiasts? *SVMRC*.

(*above*) Looking south along the 'Old Road' as 'Peak' D123 rounds the curve of the junction with a Down express. In the distance a goods train uses the south side of the triangular junction. (*below*) Rotherham Masboro' station in September 1962 with 'Peak' D76 departing with an express from Leeds to St Pancras via Sheffield. The Cricklewood 14A based locomotive was less than two years old but its external appearance was disappointing! *Both SVMRC.*

And now back to Sheffield for an indulgent treat for Deltic fans! These two pages show D9005 at Woodburn junction, Sheffield during an acceptance trial – light engine at first – from Doncaster to Sheffield and return. We haven't got a date for this event but the Type 5 plied this route travelling in the opposite direction on Thursday 25th May 1961 en route from Vulcan Foundry to Doncaster. The chances are that these images were recorded on Monday 29th May during the locomotives' first run out since being received by BR. It is early morning and the photographer must have had word that D9005 was coming over to Sheffield. Within a few weeks it would be delivered to Gateshead where that immaculate finish would soon disappear! *Both SVMRC.*

Getting the priority afforded express passenger trains, Derby based 'Peak' D22 slides out of Midland station, Sheffield in April 1962 with a Down working. Looking on, Barrow Hill 8F No.48103 has a train of empty mineral wagons. *SVMRC*.

(*above*) A crew training run for Darnall Drivers just prior to the launch of the diesel hauled Pullman services to King's Cross was being carried out using EE Type 4 D207, the chosen locomotive class for the inaugural services. D207 still has a certain amount of newness about it in this September 1958 image near Woodhouse. (*below*) Another glorious day in the suburbs of Sheffield! Are we missing a trick here? However, as the headboard informs us, this was a special working for Parkgate, Iron & Steel Co. Ltd. – 1Z10 – with Finsbury Park 34G based Brush Type 4 D1526 doing the honours. The date is unknown, the destination is unknown, as is the starting point. Dear readers.... and any information you can supply would be gratefully received. *Both SVMRC.*

(*above*) Brush D1555 en route to Rotherwood yard where electric traction will take over this coal train destined for somewhere west of the Pennines travelling via the MSW system. The date is in August 1964 when the Co-Co was allocated to Tinsley; its delivery dates were 27th February 1964 new to Darnall depot; 26th April 1964 transferred to the new depot located at the eastern end of the marshalling yard at Tinsley; 28th November 1964 moved to Stratford. (*below*) Super power for a northbound morning express departing Chesterfield in August 1961; the motive power consists fairly new Derby-built 'Peak' D40, and eight-month old Crewe-built D75. The mist – whatever its origin – has yet to clear over the town although the sun is giving it a go! *Both SVMRC.*

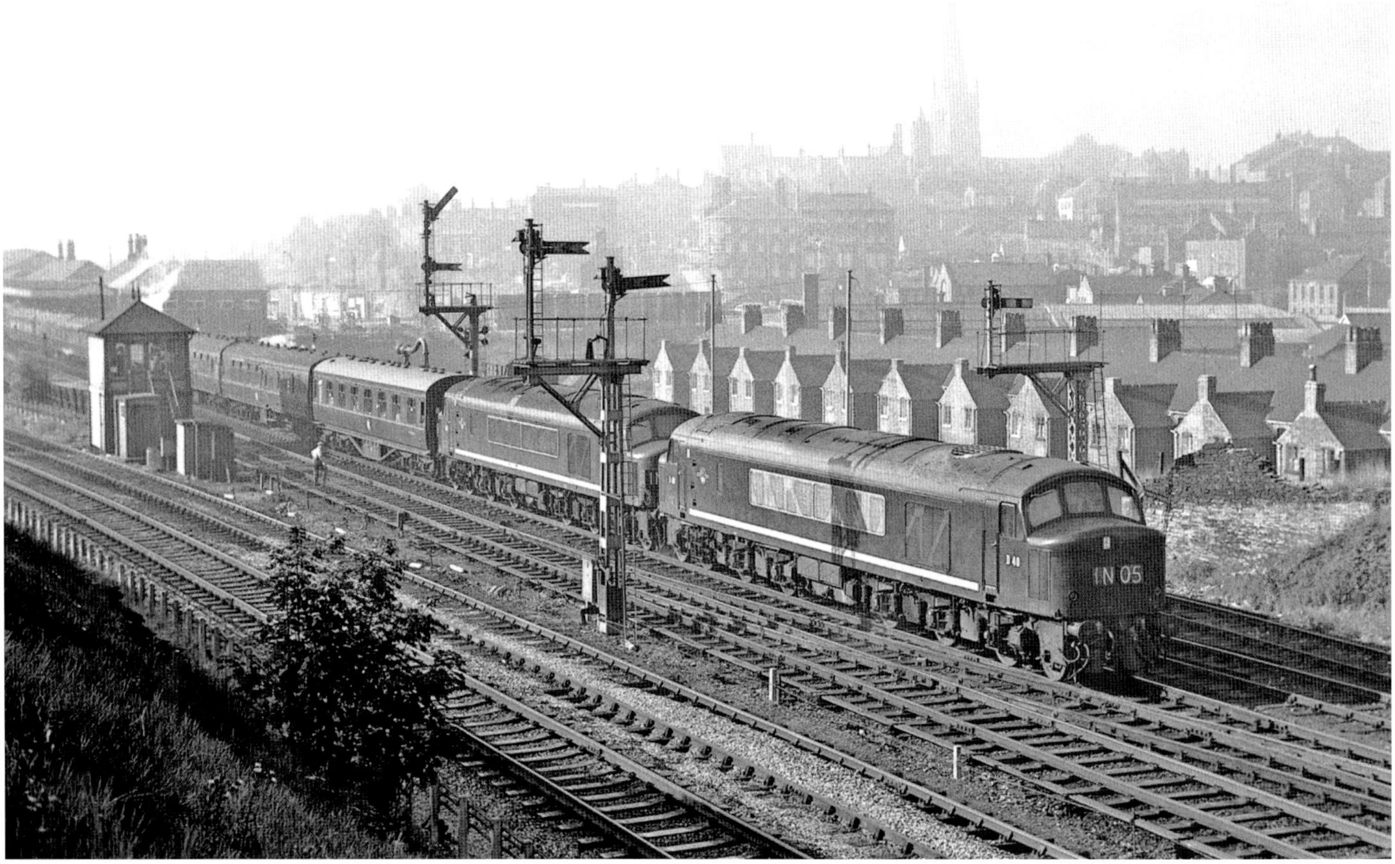

(*above*) An inter-regional passenger working – is this *THE DEVONIAN* – approaches Chesterfield with Neville Hill 'Peak' D17 in charge. This locomotive was allocated to 55H from 26th March 1961 ex Derby, to 8th December 1962 to Holbeck so this working was at some period during those twenty months with summer 1962 looking to be the favourite. (*below*) Using the Up goods line, Beyer, Peacock-built Clayton D8604 brings a train of power station coal – the stuff nobody else could burn – through Chesterfield. Originating at Seymour yard, the coal – I forgot, it was also ideal for coking too – was destined for the Avenue Coking Plant at Clay Cross; any number of collieries in the immediate area could have contributed the slack coal. This locomotive was one of the Tinsley batch which from early days – new to 41A 15th September 1964 – was sent to Barrow Hill – 5th April 1965 along with sisters D8605 to D8615; D8616 was not delivered until 23rd April 1965 so went direct to Barrow Hill – but in actuality many of them had been working from the Staveley shed since 1964. For all the hoo-hah created around this class, they performed quite well on the Eastern Region and did what was asked of them, as here. By the end of May 1966 however they had all been transferred to Scotland, replaced by EE Type 1s! *Both SVMRC.*

The mist has cleared and that amazing crooked spire is still standing; Brush D5684 heads north with a Down express as a DMU motors south on a service to Derby. The Up and Down goods by-pass lines are on the left whilst to the right of the locomotive is a scrapyard which took care of a number of steam locomotives during the great cull of the 1960s. *SVMRC*.

(*above*) Locally produced 'Peak' D40 arrives at Derby (Midland) with a Down express circa September 1961. Note the hotch-potch of rolling stock! *SVMRC*. (*below*) There comes a time! Minus its prime mover and middle wheelset, first generation diesel-electric shunter 12002 awaits its turn to be cut up at Derby in September 1956. Built for the LMS by Hawthorn Leslie, the 0-6-0DE shunter was put into traffic in April 1936 as No.7079 at Crewe South depot from where it worked for the whole of its life. It was withdrawn at Derby on 16th June 1956 after arrival for overhaul; it had put in some twenty years faithful service and had proved the viability of its ilk. *PL/BLP*.

MORE ON THE WESTERN REGION

(*above*) Four of the NBL built B-B Type 2 diesel-hydraulics stand by the fuelling rack at Laira depot in 1964; only D6315 and D6301 are identifiable. Of these, three of them had been fitted with the twin headcode box – D6334 onwards were built with them – which was retro-fitted in the earlier locomotives. All of this class except Nos.D6336, D6337 – Newton Abbot; D6347, and D6354 to D6357 Bath Road, all went new to the Plymouth depot and of those mentioned at least three of them were also allocated to Laira at some point during their short lives. By February 1972 all of them had been condemned and none – mercifully some might say – were preserved! BLP. (*below*) The summer evening sun bathes the body side of B-B 'Warship' D802 FORMIDABLE at Penzance in June 1959. This particular member of the class put in less than ten years of service! *PL/BLP*.

(*above*) En route to somewhere in England, Landore based D1005 WESTERN VENTURER runs through Severn Tunnel Junction station with a fitted freight in 1968. (*below*) Another Landore 'Western' D1025 WESTERN GUARDSMAN enters Swansea (High Street) in 1969. *Both BLP*.

(*above*) Laira Type 4 'Warship' D835 PEGASUS languishes at Swindon awaiting works attention in 1961. Note the 83D shed plate fixed to the bufferbeam just above the vacuum pipe. The four-character route indicators were introduced from D812 onwards, and D800 to D811 were fitted with them by 1963. The DMU behind appears new – a three-car cross-country Swindon built class 120? - but we have no records of its car numbers. The gas works in the background was all part of the GWR set-up at Swindon. SVMRC. (*below*) They even had to have a different shade of green for the cab! A new D9500 outside the workshops at Swindon in June 1964, before the 0-6-0DHs 8th July release to traffic at Bath Road. Copious amounts of yellow paint had been applied to those areas deemed as requiring highlighting. It was as though the WR were trying to create the perfect trip and shunting locomotive. If they had chosen electric transmission instead of hydraulic then who knows what the locomotive might have achieved. However, it wasn't all about that transmission with this class it was its role in the great scheme where trip working for instance was fast disappearing as BR was losing business at a rate similar to the High Street retail outlets of the 2010s. The creation of the class did keep a few hundred skilled artificers in work for a few years but that was about its only positive; or was that the prime intention of the authorities? *PL/BLP*.

(*above*) The crew of a mixed freight seem determined to have their faces recorded along with 'Hymek' D7050 at Pilning on 16th May 1964. The train would soon be entering the Severn tunnel en route to South Wales. (*below*) Big power, small load! Three empty milk tankers and a bogie brake van with only a guard aboard do not constitute a trial for 2,700 h.p. Heading west, D1046 WESTERN MARQUIS threads Sonning cutting on 28th March 1965. *PL/BLP*.

(*above*) This is what they were partly made for; D6330 with a three-coach formation near Yeovil (Town) on 18th May 1964 working a service from Taunton. (*below*) Yes another DMU – W51084 is the first car – squeezes into the album. This one was working out of Yeovil (Town) on a Bristol-Weymouth service on 18th May 1964. *Both PL/BLP*.

A change of scenery now!(*above*) Working empty stock from Paddington to Old Oak Common, D6352 has reached the gas works on the east side of Mitre Bridge from where this image was recorded on 7th October 1965. This B-B managed to get around a bit during its rather short lifetime: New to Laira in July 1962, it was transferred to Bristol on 6th October 1962, then Old Oak on 14th September 1964. It was broken up at Swindon during November 1971. (*below*) Mitre Bridge again with 'Hymek' D7067 working an eastbound parcels train on 18th April 1964. *Both PL/BLP*.

(*above*) Passing beneath Mitre Bridge in may 1962 'Warship' D858 VALOROUS heads a Bristol (Temple Meads)-London (Paddington) express. (*below*) Later during that same June morning in May 1962 'Hymek' D7021 brings another express in from Bristol. Barely four months old, the B-B is looking rather unkempt; at least the coaching stock was clean. *Both PL/BLP*.

(*above*) Another February 1962 built diesel locomotive! D1001 WESTERN PATHFINDER runs towards Paddington with an express from Birmingham in June 1962. (*below*) It wasn't all sunshine and flowers on the WR main line. On a cold 29th December 1962 – in the depth of that long and vicious winter – 'Hymek' D7017 heads west out of London with a parcels train. Hopefully the cab heaters were working aboard D7017 but hats off to the photographer for venturing out and recording this minor event. *Both PL/BLP.*

There could be any number of reasons why 'Hymek' D7000 was being lifted from its running gear at Swindon in the summer of 1961 but the presence of a senior fitter, a man in a gabardine Mack along with a couple of people approaching the B-B wearing suits leads one to believe it may have been something serious or simply an inspection taking place. We are looking at the 'B' end of the locomotive where the hydraulic equipment and coolant group was located; note the two fuel tanks have been taken off and put to one side. 'Warship' D601 ACTIVE – before it was fitted with split box route indicators – shares the bay. There was something ironic about the locomotives' name but I can't quite ...... *SVMRC*

When it was new! D602 BULLDOG being coupled-up at Swindon in December 1958 whilst undergoing acceptance trials which included working service trains such as this. Note the cheery smile from the Driver. This was one of the trio which were sent to work in South Wales and although allocated to Landore, the three worked mainly from Margam and Pantyffynnon. According to one former WR Traction Controller it was the Route availability which cut short their stay in Wales. However, the same man was GWR through and through so he would defend them anyway! *PL/BLP*.

(*above*) 'Warship' D825 INTREPID accelerates away from Taunton in October 1963 with a Down express. The station can be seen in the background, the last carriage having just left platform 5. (*below*) Not quite sure what is happening here but C-C 'Warship' D602 COSSACK and B-B 'Warship' D823 HERMES are out on the main line at Swindon on a date yet to be recorded. The three original 'Warships' which ventured into South Wales looking for work were all returned to Laira during late November 1967; D601 and D602 on 22nd whilst D604 managed the run back to Plymouth on the 24th! The five members of the original 'Warship' class were withdrawn en masse on the last day of 1967 at Laira depot where they were stored prior to their final journey to the two Welsh scrapyards which cut them. Only two of the class – D600 and D602 – were ever painted in blue livery, the others retaining the Brunswick green of delivery. All five were fitted with the split type route indicator boxes later in life and all but D600 had the small yellow warning panel painted on each end. *Both SVMRC.*

Off to Hatton now where a number of trains serving the West Midlands are captured negotiating the junctions north of the station. (*above*) Old Oak Common 'Brush' Type 4 D1694 clears the East junction and runs through the station at Hatton – change for Stratford-on-Avon – with an Up inter-regional express during the summer of 1964. One of the Brush-built members of the class, reaching BR metals in December 1963, this locomotive became 47106 under TOPs and ended its days at Tinsley depot working coal trains when Yorkshire still had mines bringing that precious commodity to the surface. It was condemned in February 1988 and cut up at Vic Berry's yard in Leicester. (*below*) A Down express in the care of another Old Oak based Brush-built 'Brush' – D1707 – runs over the East junction at Hatton and heads towards Birmingham. This locomotive too was withdrawn in 1988 but in the December from Cardiff Canton as 47487. *Both SVMRC.*

(*above*) Leaving Hatton station in its wake, 'Western' D1010 WESTERN CAMPAIGNER negotiates the East junction just west of the station whilst working an express from Paddington to Snow Hill in 1964. (*below*) Oxley based 'Brush' D1689 takes the Warwick route at Hatton North junction with an unidentified Up working in August 1964. *Both SVMRC.*

(*above*) Being given the road for the Warwick line, Leicester based BR Sulzer Type 2 D7579 heads south and then east, and eventually home, with a fitted van train during the summer of 1964. (*below*) Standing in the gloom of the tunnel mouth at the western end of Birmingham's (Snow Hill) station, one of the Western Region's diesel Pullman sets has just arrived at platform 5 during the summer of 1961. This would have been the 1650 departure 'Birmingham Pullman' from London (Paddington) due at 1850 and we are looking at Motor Brake Second W60094 which had seats for eighteen passengers, a Guard's compartment for luggage, an engine room for the V12 North British/M.A.N. 1,000 h.p. engine, along with a full width driving compartment, all enclosed in 66ft long body and weighing in at 67 tons 10 cwt with bogies. At the other end of the eight-car unit it was the same; in between the two driving trailers were six assorted parlour and kitchen cars. The WR had three of these 8-car units the LMR had two six-car trains. All were introduced in September 1960. *Both SVMRC.*

With uniforms akin to those worn by ice-cream salesmen of the era! The Driver and Secondman of a WR Pullman diesel service between Wolverhampton and London peer through the windows of their charge in June 1962 as the unit negotiates the North junction at Hatton and heads towards Warwick en route to Paddington. The final service of 'The Birmingham Pullman' from Snow Hill ran on Friday 3rd March 1967. The following Monday New Street station became the major terminus for London services from Birmingham via the newly electrified and speeded up WCML. It wasn't quite the end for the diesel Pullman sets though as all five – the LMR 'Midland Pullman' sets were also displaced by the WCML upgrade – were employed by the Western Region on services to South Wales, and Bristol. However, by 1973 they were all withdrawn as BR's Mk.2 air-conditioned stock gave a better ride without the Pullman supplement! *SVMRC*.

Hatton North junction looking south-east from the footbridge as an unidentified 'Western' approaches on the Warwick line with an express from Paddington. The secondary route to Stratford, heading off towards the south-west, is decidedly weed grown compared with the main line. *SVMRC*.

SOUTHERN REGION – THE TYPE 3s & OTHER MOTIVE POWER

(*top*) BRC&W Type 3 D6532 runs through the shallow rock cutting at Bearstead & Thurnham en route to Ashford with the 0910 Charing Cross to Margate service on Friday 12th May 1961. (*above*) Later that same morning, also at Bearstead & Thurnham, D6513 works the 1100 Charing Cross-Margate. The route taken by these two trains, via Ashford and Wye amounted to a total distance of 91 miles covered. *Both PL/BLP.*

(*above*) The 0550 ex-Bromford Bridge empty tanks nears Wallers Ash tunnel north of Winchester en route to Fawley oil refinery on 10th July 1965. (*below*) It all looks rather heritage but it's not! Brand new – to traffic 4th November 1961 at Hither Green – D6575 heads an Up tank train at Stoke Junction Halt on the Isle-of-Grain on a splendid November morning in 1961. Passenger services on this branch were withdrawn from Monday 4th December 1961 and this halt became history; the goods trains however continue today. *Both PL/BLP.*

A double-take at Bournemouth (Central) in 1965! (*above*) D6573 heads a westbound afternoon goods train and is waiting in the middle road for a signal. (*below*) Just over an hour later that afternoon sister D6526, looking rather smart and no doubt ex-works, has a strange load in tow in the shape of a Stanier Class 5 4-6-0. Two young 'spotters have noticed the rarity and are trying to look up its number in their Southern Region Ian Allan ABC! *Both SVMRC.*

(*above*) Passing the junction to Salisbury at Redbridge, D6575 greets us again whilst working another tank train – loaded ex-Fawley – to an unknown destination on 28th March 1966. (*below*) Former Southern Railway 350 h.p. 0-6-0DE shunter No.15201 stands at the fuelling point at Norwood Junction shed circa 1959 with one of the BR 350 h.p. 0-6-0DEs for company. The rudimentary facilities provided for the diesel locomotives at Norwood Junction look more reminiscent to a temporary farm yard set-up rather than a permanent purpose-built affair providing fuel for forty or so allocated diesel shunters. Using gravity to help the situation, the fuelling point was located opposite the end of the elevated line from the coal stage – where upon a tank wagon was placed – just in front of the turntable. Put to traffic in September 1937 by the Southern as their No.1, this locomotive was one of a trio built at Ashford – the others were 2 and 3 which went to work in September and October 1937 respectively. Renumbered by BR, this 0-6-0DE was withdrawn in November 1964 from Eastleigh. Its two sisters became 15202 and 15203 and were taken out of service at about the same time. None of the three shunters remained loyal to Norwood Junction depot but 15203 returned to the shed shortly before withdrawal. *PL/BLP*.

Two views of 15203, the only prodigal which returned home to Norwood Junction. Here on 11th May 1963 the 0-6-0DE shunter was looking rather worn-out and no doubt its mechanics were in need of renewal after twenty-six years of work. It was withdrawn 29th November 1964 with sister 15201 whilst 15202 survived two more weeks. It was with sister 15202 that this shunter went on loan to the Western Region at Old Oak Common from 12th May 1951 to 24th October 1953 when the pair returned to Norwood. Finally, it is worth a quick comparison with the BR version of the 350 h.p. 0-6-0DE which weighed in at approximately 49 tons whereas this trio came in at 55 tons each; it must have been those large fuel tanks! *PL/BLP*.